FORMULA 1
HANDBOOK
2023

Guymer

GRAND PRIX GUIDE

FOR F1 FANS

Introduction

Congratulations on your purchase of

the 2nd book in the formula 1 handbook series:

FORMULA 1 HANDBOOK 2023 GRAND PRIX GUIDE FOR F1 FANS

If you're an avid F1 fan like us, this handbook will be a handy reference throughout the Championship Season, providing a 2022 review, 2023 preview and all the important facts & stats of your favourite drivers, teams, and tracks. Scan the points table QR code for an updated PDF version of results after each race, take notes and collect autographs at the track. We hope you enjoy this book, and the uniquely crafted caricatures by Chloe Guymer (@fineartschloe on Instagram). If you do make sure to tell your friends about it!

AND IT'S GO, GO, GO !!!

Murray Walker 1923 – 2021

TABLE OF CONTENTS

2022 REVIEW

It was always going to be difficult to surpass the dizzying heights of 2021 which saw Max Verstappen claim his first title in acrimonious circumstances, though anticipation for the new season was at fever pitch with the advent of a new set of regulations which promised to shake up the long established status quo.

When Ferrari made good on this with a dominant 1-2 at the Bahrain curtain raiser, whilst Red Bull battled reliability issues in the opening races alongside the unusual sight of Mercedes adrift of the pace following eight seasons at the top, there was genuine hope that the Prancing Horse was on the way to restoring its' former glory. These expectations proved folly, as Ferrari ultimately doubled their victory tally of two from the first three events across the balance of the season. Despite boasting a formidable twelve pole positions, nine of which were claimed by Charles Leclerc, they fell into old ways on the strategic front, coupled with reliability woes which frequently occurred whilst in a commanding position.

Carlos Sainz's maiden victory at Silverstone was a highlight, though the unrealised potential and relentless blame culture at Maranello culminated in Mattia Binotto falling on his sword following four seasons as team principal. Once their own reliability gremlins were sorted, Red Bull rapidly emerged as the team to beat, as reigning champion Verstappen went on a tear to claim eight victories before the mid-season break and place one hand on another crown. The Dutchman, who secured the title in Japan with four races to spare, would go on to break the season win tally record at fifteen. Alongside team-mate Sergio Perez's two victories, the team won 75% of races, rivalling Mercedes' strike rate during its peak dominance.

Having taken a misstep with the regulation overhaul, Mercedes spent much of the season clawing back the initial deficit which initially consigned them from being in contention to win almost every race since 2014, to fighting for podiums only when Ferrari or Red Bull encountered issues. By the second half of the season, they were providing headaches for Red Bull and beating Ferrari more often than not. Whilst Lewis Hamilton would endure the first winless campaign of his career, team-mate George Russell broke through for his maiden triumph at Brazil, leading Hamilton home for a 1-2 which signalled that the Silver Arrows will be back in the title hunt in 2023.

Further down the grid, four time World Champion Sebastian Vettel, who missed the first two races due to COVID, announced his retirement following fifteen seasons, with two forgettable seasons at Aston Martin a disappointing footnote to a career which began so successfully. The German will be replaced by old title sparring partner and another ex-Ferrari alum in Fernando Alonso, who ran out of patience following two years at Alpine.

Another driver falling off the grid is Daniel Ricciardo, after enduring a wretched two season McLaren tenure, notwithstanding his memorable victory at Monza in 2021, with both parties mutually agreeing to conclude the partnership twelve months early. The Australian will re-join Red Bull, where he enjoyed the majority of his success, as a reserve driver next season. His compatriot, Oscar Piastri, steps into a drive at McLaren following a protracted legal battle over his services with Alpine.

Mick Schumacher found himself out of a drive at season's end despite regularly outperforming team-mate Kevin Magnussen at Haas. After a costly early season crash during qualifying at Saudi Arabia which saw him sit out the race and another at a wet Monaco, he broke through for points at Britain and Austria. However, amidst increasingly unfavourable strategic calls, the German's surname wasn't enough to convince Guenther Steiner to retain him for a third season, with his compatriot, Nico Hulkenberg, returning to the sport in a full-time capacity for the first time since 2019.

In 2022 there were on average 1.21 million viewers per race, with 521,000 18-49 year olds tuning in (up by 29%) whilst 36,000 12 to 17 year old viewership represented the biggest demographic increase up by a massive 49%. Women made up 28% of the audience (up by 34%) with 352,000 women watching the increasingly popular motorsport.

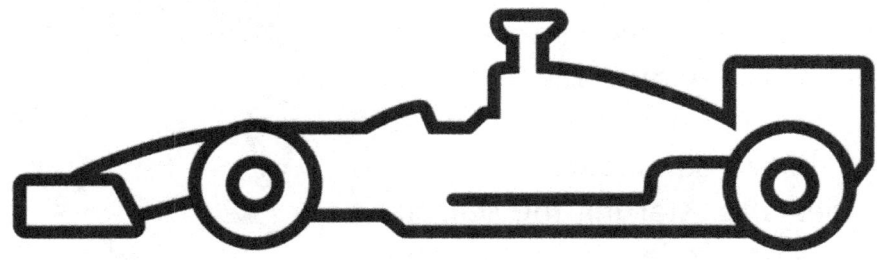

2023 PREVIEW

Despite China's cancellation for a fourth consecutive year and its' vacant slot remaining unfilled, Formula One embarks on its' longest season in 2023 with a record 23 events. The sport's expansion into North America, bolstered by the sustained success of 'Drive to Survive', sees Las Vegas join the calendar after Miami's arrival last season. Qatar returns after featuring for the first time in 2021, with the Paul Ricard circuit in France a casualty having only resurfaced in 2018.

Following a solitary pre-season test at Bahrain, the grid reconvenes at the same venue to commence proceedings. The three-day test indicated that reigning champions, Red Bull, with their future beyond 2025 secure having announced a partnership with Ford, remain the team to beat, whilst Max Verstappen seems more relaxed than ever after claiming his second title, though the pecking order behind them appears uncertain.

Testing also suggests that Ferrari has produced a fast yet temperamental car, which will do little to quell the uncertainty that manifested in 2022, when the Prancing Horse squandered countless opportunities after starting the season as the team to beat. Frederic Vasseur's arrival as Team Principal, reuniting him with Charles Leclerc following their time

together at Sauber (now Alfa Romeo) in 2018, will provide a fascinating backdrop to any political machinations stemming from on track fortunes as the Maranello outfit are wont to.

Mercedes cannot be dismissed after a season consigned to best of the rest status behind Red Bull and Ferrari on the back of eight consecutive titles, having returned to the top step of the podium in Brazil with George Russell leading home Lewis Hamilton for a 1-2, and on the basis of testing, solving the porpoising issues which decimated their 2022 campaign, though a permanent return to the front of the field this soon appears unlikely. At 38, Hamilton will want evidence of inroads sooner than later prior to committing to what will surely represent the final contract of his storied career.

Aston Martin raised the most eyebrows after producing impressive times over long mileage, fuelling hopes that Fernando Alonso's decision to depart Alpine following two frustrating seasons will pay dividends. Lance Stroll's mysterious accident on the eve of testing, which resulted in wrist injuries that denied the Canadian the opportunity to take to the car across the three days and placed his presence on the grid for the opening races in doubt, will allow Alonso to assert his authority on the team from the outset.

Alpine now boasts two French compatriots, with Pierre Gasly joining Esteban Ocon from Alpha Tauri, and their development as the season progresses will be fascinating to witness considering the pair has enjoyed a colourful history dating back to their time in the junior formulae.

McLaren replaced one Australian with another after jettisoning Daniel Ricciardo on the back of two disappointing seasons, with the seven-time victor returning to his happy hunting ground at Red Bull in a reserve and promotional role. In his place, Oscar Piastri makes his debut, following an acrimonious battle for his services with Alpine, who announced Piastri, then serving in a reserve capacity at the French outfit, as one of their drivers for 2023 after Fernando Alonso confirmed his departure for Aston Martin, only for the Australian to deny the announcement, leading to the legal tussle in which McLaren eventually prevailed.

Lando Norris' patience will be tested if the momentum which McLaren had been building until last season, which saw him on the cusp of becoming a Grand Prix winner several times in 2021, isn't renewed. Having committed his immediate future to the Woking outfit and proving his credentials after enjoying Ricciardo's measure throughout their tenure as team-mates, the Briton, entering his fifth season, will be in high demand should he attempt to extricate himself from the team.

Andreas Seidl's defection from McLaren to become Alfa Romeo's CEO ahead of the Swiss outfit's transition into Audi was a coup, and his ties to McLaren could prove interesting in the future. Valtteri Bottas appears more relaxed than ever over twelve months removed from the spotlight he endured throughout his five season Mercedes tenure. The Finn kept himself occupied cycling in Australia, where his professional cyclist girlfriend hails from, and New Zealand during the off season, adopting a larrikin persona and claiming the 'iconic' Victoria Bitter (sharing the same initials) beer as his own during his time Down Under, which endeared him to many across social media. Nevertheless, the ten time winner will remain keen to prove that he wishes to be a part of the team's long term future with works status, and his time at a manufacturer with Mercedes' pedigree could prove advantageous.

Guymer

In their final season under the Alfa Romeo moniker, the Sauber controlled outfit (which will officially become Audi from 2026 after the German marque by way of parent company Volkswagen) finally committed to entering the sport and will seek greater consistency after its' form fell away following a strong start.

Haas ruthlessly discarded Mick Schumacher after two seasons, with the son of seven time champion, Michael, falling out of favour following multiple self-inflicted crashes early in the season. Despite registering points at Britain and Austria and being on the wrong end of several questionable strategic decisions, the damage had been done and the German has been replaced by his compatriot, Nico Hulkenberg, who returns to the grid in a full-time capacity for the first time since 2019. Kevin Magnussen returns following his career resurrection on the eve of last season at Nikita Mazepin's expense in the wake of the Russia-Ukraine conflict. The Dane will be keen to assert himself over Hulkenberg, with the pair forming one of the oldest combinations on the grid.

Alpha Tauri will be seeking a return to regular points with Nyck de Vries' arrival. The Dutchman impressed when he deputised for Williams' Alexander Albon at Monza, finishing ninth. Logan Sargeant joins Albon at Williams in place of Nicholas Latifi, becoming the first American to compete in the sport since Alexander Rossi in 2015.

2023 TECH TORQUE

Introduction

Whilst changes to specs and regulations for the 2023 F1 World Championship aren't as significant as those were for the Covid Pandemic afflicted 2022 season, the FIA is continuing its' drive to boost F1 popularity and profit via ramping up competition and overtaking between teams, evidenced most recently by the addition of a fourth DRS zone at the Melbourne Grand Prix. Alongside this, is a continued focus on driver comfort and safety, particularly in relation to the roll hoop, following Zhou Guanyu's death defying crash at Silverstone, and further attempts to eliminate the vertical oscillation 'porpoising' effect brought about by the focus on ground force effects.

Roll Hoops

The shape of roll hoops, which sit on top of the chassis and behind the driver, has been overhauled with a more rounded top being mandated to increase driver safety during rollovers and prevent the digging in and spectacular flipping that occurred during Guanyu's first corner carnage at the start of the 2022 British Grand Prix. In this heart-stopping incident, the Alfa Romeo's blade shaped roll hoop dug into the gravel-trap and was actually torn off, with the halo being the only component resting between Zhou's head and the tarmac. As a result, the FIA has increased the roll hoop's strength requirements and minimum height for the regulatory homologation (derived from the Greek word *homologeo* for 'I agree') test point, that will be monitored by a specific sensor, and has introduced a new physical test on horizontal forward motion loads on the hoop, with a focus on sudden high impact loads. The FIA may also have to consider increasing the contact area between the monocoque (survivor cell) and roll hoop to prevent the dangerous disconnect that took place in Silverstone. Whilst these changes will impact on each team's budget, they are obviously in the driver's best interests. The cost cap per team is expected to drop from $142.4 million to $135 million due to lower than expected inflation rates. Accident damage allowance has been doubled and fixed at $300k per team for each weekend that includes a sprint.

Aerodynamics & Bodywork

The FIA has 'upped the ante' on the ground effect aerodynamics which were reintroduced in 2022, designed to increase downforce and grip for both leading and chasing cars on straights, facilitating slipstreaming, whilst reducing detrimental drag and wake/turbulence effects during cornering. Floor edges have been raised this year by 15mm to reduce air stalling under the chassis which has been causing a very uncomfortable, noisy and potentially dangerous porpoising on straights, combined with additional sensors and more stringent flex tests on floor elasticity to ensure adherence to this rule. Similarly, the height of the diffuser throat, which is the lowest section of the wind tunnel, has been raised and its edge stiffened to optimize airflow.

There has been a reduction in minimum car weight, 2kg down from 2022 to 796kg (sans fuel and driver) and an emphasis on sleek side pods to reduce drag. Side pods interact with the floor and rear wing to direct and cool air towards the engine, and also impact upon floor flexibility. In 2023, the F1 teams are taking different approaches to this technology. Mercedes has adopted a slimline 'zeropod' strategy, whilst Ferrari and other teams have chosen either 'upwash' or 'downwash' models that displace and direct air in opposite directions.

Rear vision mirrors have been increased to improve driver visibility with the width of the reflective surface increasing from 150 to 200mm, however this has increased drag, so teams are looking for other ways to offset this effect. With strakes (front wing slot gap separators) no longer needing to be "primarily" for mechanical, structural or measurement reasons, Ferrari, much to Mercedes' chagrin, have fitted ten cleverly engineered strakes on its new SF23 front wing design, that, no matter how much of an aerodynamic boost they provide, are now permitted. It remains to be seen if Mercedes or the other teams follow suit.

The sliding scale in relation to wind tunnel testing and Computational Fluid Dynamics (CFD) that enables aerodynamic simulations combined with complex mathematical computations to predict airflow has continued with less successful teams being awarded proportionately more time to increase their competitiveness. There are six aerodynamic testing periods (ATP) in a championship season with an average of 320 wind tunnel runs (where airspeed rises and falls above and below 5m per second) plus 80 hours of 'on wind' time (time spent with airspeed above 15mps) per team, totaling 400 hours within the wind tunnel per team.

2023 TECH TORQUE

Gearbox

Modifications when materials, processes or proprietary parts become available are now permitted, when clear documentation justifying the change has been provided, prior approval granted and no performance advantage is gained, with all teams being notified of the changes.

Fuel

Fuel temperature must be higher than either 10 degrees centigrade below ambient temperature, or 10 (instead of 20) degrees centigrade, giving teams more flexibility to cool fuel.

Qualifying Format, Tyres, and DRS Trials

Two events will have revised qualifying formats (RQF) to evaluate the suitability of revisions for subsequent championships. Tyres will be provided solely by Pirelli and will allow for a maximum of 11 sets (instead of 13) of dry-weather(slick) tyres: Q1 - hard tyres only (red branding with and without brackets), Q2 – medium tyres only (yellow branding with brackets), Q3 – soft tyres only (white branding with and without brackets). If the RQF sessions are declared wet, intermediate (4 sets with green branding and brackets) and wets (3 sets with blue branding and brackets) will be permitted.

Drag Reduction System (DRS) activation is to be evaluated via trials in each sprint session and based on the results may be brought forward by 1 lap at the start of a race/sprint or after restarts in all races in 2024.

2023 TECH TORQUE

Parc Fermé and Curfew Rules

Parc fermé means 'closed park' in French and this secure area is used in F1 to quarantine cars so that only minor adjustments may be made between qualifying and race day. There will be a review of parc fermé rules on sprint weekends to simplify the set-up locking process and reduce parc fermé requests between qualifying and sprint sessions. There will also be a reduction in the number of hours F1 team members are allowed to work, with curfews coming into place up to two times earlier than before.

Grid Penalties

These regulations have been, and will continue to be, updated following 2022's Italian Grand Prix in which many teams sustained gearbox and power unit drops, causing a confusing order reshuffle. The FIA regulations now state that "Classified drivers who have accrued more than 15 cumulative grid position penalties, or who have been penalized to start at the back of the grid, will start behind any other classified driver. Their relative position will be determined in accordance with their qualifying classification".

For those of you who are really into the technical side of F1, check out this link to the FIA's 183-page official 2023 Technical Regulations:

https://www.fia.com/sites/default/files/fia_2023_formula_1 _technical_regulations_-_issue_4_-_2022-12-07.pdf

2023 FORMULA ONE CALENDAR

R	EVENT	DATE	POLE	F.LAP	VICTOR	C.LEADER
1	BAHRAIN	MAR 5				
2	SAUDI ARABIA	MAR 19				
3	AUSTRALIA	APR 12				
4	AZERBAIJAN	APR 30				
5	MIAMI	MAY 7				
6	*EMILIA ROMAGNA*	*MAY 21*	X	X	X	X
7	MONACO	MAY 28				
8	SPAIN	JUN 4				
9	CANADA	JUN 18				
10	AUSTRIA	JUL 2				
11	BRITAIN	JUL 9				
12	HUNGARY	JUL 23				
13	BELGIUM	JUL 30				
14	NETHERLANDS	AUG 27				
15	ITALY	SEP 3				
16	SINGAPORE	SEP 17				
17	JAPAN	SEP 24				
18	QATAR	OCT 8				
19	UNITED STATES	OCT 22				
20	MEXICO CITY	OCT 29				
21	SAO PAULO	NOV 5				
22	**LAS VEGAS**	NOV 18				
23	ABU DHABI	NOV 26				

Bold = new event   Italics = cancelled event

2023 FORMULA ONE GRID

RED BULL HONDA
1. Max Verstappen (NED)

2022 CHAMPION

11. Sergio Perez (MEX)

MERCEDES
44. Lewis Hamilton (GBR)

63. George Russell (GBR)

McLAREN MERCEDES
4. Lando Norris (GBR)

81. Oscar Piastri (AUS) **(R)**

ASTON MARTIN MERCEDES
14. Fernando Alonso (ESP)

18. Lance Stroll (CAN)

ALPHATAURI HONDA
21. Nyck De Vries (NED) **(R)**

22. Yuki Tsunoda (JAP)

FERRARI
16. Charles Leclerc (MON)

55. Carlos Sainz (ESP)

ALPINE RENAULT
10. Pierre Gasly (FRA)

31. Esteban Ocon (FRA)

ALFA ROMEO FERRARI
24. Zhou Guanyu (CHN)

77. Valtteri Bottas (FIN)

HAAS FERRARI
20. Kevin Magnussen (DEN)

27. Nico Hulkenberg (DEU)

WILLIAMS MERCEDES
2. Logan Sargeant (USA) **(R)**

23. Alex Albon (THA)

As has been the case since 2010, the top ten drivers are awarded points, whilst an additional point is awarded to the driver & constructor setting the fastest lap, **provided they finish inside the top ten**. After each race, use this points guide & table (overleaf) to record drivers' & constructors' points. Use the wider columns to include sprint results. Tally these in the final columns or simply scan the QR Code above to receive an updated PDF version of race/sprint & championship results after each race.

POSITION	RACE POINTS	SPRINT POINTS
1st:	25	8
2nd:	18	7
3rd:	15	6
4th:	12	5
5th:	10	4
6th:	8	3
7th:	6	2
8th:	4	1
9th:	2	
10th:	1	

* Fastest Lap: 1 point

** Winner

DNF Did not finish

2023 RACE POINTS TABLE

CONS	DRIVER	BAH	SAU	AUS	AZE	MIA	EMI	MON	SPA	CAN	AUT	GBR
RED BULL	VERSTAPPEN						X					
RED BULL	PEREZ						X					
FERRARI	LECLERC						X					
FERRARI	SAINZ						X					
MERCEDES	RUSSELL						X					
MERCEDES	HAMILTON						X					
ALPINE	OCON						X					
ALPINE	GASLY						X					
McLAREN	NORRIS						X					
McLAREN	PIASTRI						X					
ALFA ROMEO	BOTTAS						X					
ALFA ROMEO	ZHOU						X					
ASTON MARTIN	ALONSO						X					
ASTON MARTIN	STROLL						X					
HAAS	MAGNUSSEN						X					
HAAS	HULKENBERG						X					
ALPHA TAURI	TSUNODA						X					
ALPHA TAURI	DE VRIES						X					
WILLIAMS	ALBON						X					
WILLIAMS	SARGEANT						X					

2023 RACE POINTS TABLE

HUN	BEL	NED	ITA	SIN	JAP	QAT	USA	MEX	SAO	LV	ABU	DRV POS	PTS	CON POS	PTS

YOUR TOP 3 PREDICTIONS FOR 2023

DRIVER'S CHAMPIONSHIP

....

....

....

CONSTRUCTOR'S CHAMPIONSHIP

....

....

....

RED BULL RBPT

Debut:	2005
Races:	347
Pole Positions:	81
Victories:	92
Drivers Championships:	6
Constructors:	5

1. MAX VERSTAPPEN — Netherlands

DOB:	30/9/97
Debut:	2015
Races:	163
Pole Positions:	20
Podiums:	77
Victories:	35
Championships:	2

11. SERGIO PEREZ — Mexico

DOB:	26/1/90
Debut:	2011
Races:	235
Pole Positions:	1
Podiums:	26
Victories:	4
Championships:	N/A

FERRARI

Debut:	1950
Races:	1051
Pole Positions:	242
Victories:	241
Drivers Championships:	15
Constructors:	16

16. CHARLES LECLERC — Monaco

DOB:	16/10/97
Debut:	2018
Races:	102
Pole Positions:	18
Podiums:	24
Victories:	5
Championships:	N/A

55. CARLOS SAINZ — Spain

DOB:	1/9/94
Debut:	2015
Races:	162
Pole Positions:	3
Podiums:	15
Victories:	1
Championships:	N/A

MERCEDES

Debut:	1954 (re-entered 2010)
Races:	271
Pole Positions:	136
Victories:	125
Drivers Championships:	9
Constructors:	8

44. LEWIS HAMILTON	**Great Britain**
DOB:	7/1/85
Debut:	2007
Races:	310
Pole Positions:	103
Podiums:	191
Victories:	103
Championships:	7

63. GEORGE RUSSELL	**Great Britain**
DOB:	15/2/98
Debut:	2019
Races:	82
Pole Positions:	1
Podiums:	9
Victories:	1
Championships:	N/A

ALPINE RENAULT

Debut:	2021
Races:	44
Pole Positions:	0
Victories:	1
Drivers Championships:	0
Constructors:	0

10. PIERRE GASLY　　France

DOB:	7/2/96
Debut:	2017
Races:	108
Pole Positions:	0
Podiums:	3
Victories:	1
Championships:	N/A

31. ESTEBAN OCON　　France

DOB:	17/9/96
Debut:	2016
Races:	111
Pole Positions:	0
Podiums:	2
Victories:	1
Championships:	N/A

MCLAREN MERCEDES

Debut:	1966
Races:	924
Victories:	183
Pole Positions:	156
Drivers Championships:	12
Constructors:	8

4. LANDO NORRIS — Great Britain

DOB:	13/11/99
Debut:	2019
Races:	82
Pole Positions:	1
Podiums:	6
Victories:	0
Championships:	N/A

81. OSCAR PIASTRI — Australia

DOB:	6/4/01
Debut:	2023
Races:	0
Pole Positions:	0
Podiums:	0
Victories:	0
Championships:	N/A

ALFA ROMEO FERRARI

Debut:	1950 (re-entered 2019)
Races:	192
Pole Positions:	12
Victories:	10
Drivers Championships:	2
Constructors:	N/A

24. ZHOU GUANYU	China
DOB:	30/5/99
Debut:	2022
Races:	22
Pole Positions:	0
Podiums:	0
Victories:	0
Championships:	N/A

77. VALTTERI BOTTAS	Finland
DOB:	28/8/89
Debut:	2013
Races:	200
Pole Positions:	20
Podiums:	67
Victories:	10
Championships:	N/A

ASTON MARTIN MERCEDES

Debut:	1959 (re-entered 2021)
Races:	49
Pole Positions:	0
Victories:	0
Drivers Championships:	0
Constructors:	0

14. FERNANDO ALONSO Spain

DOB:	29/7/81
Debut:	2001
Races:	355
Pole Positions:	22
Podiums:	98
Victories:	32
Championships:	2

18. LANCE STROLL Canada

DOB:	29/10/98
Debut:	2017
Races:	122
Pole Positions:	1
Podiums:	3
Victories:	0
Championships:	N/A

HAAS FERRARI

Debut:	2016
Races:	144
Pole Positions:	1
Victories:	0
Drivers Championships:	0
Constructors:	N/A

20. KEVIN MAGNUSSEN — Denmark

DOB:	5/10/92
Debut:	2014
Races:	141
Pole Positions:	1
Podiums:	1
Victories:	0
Championships:	N/A

27. NICO HULKENBERG — Germany

DOB:	19/8/87
Debut:	2010
Races:	181
Pole Positions:	1
Podiums:	0
Victories:	0
Championships:	N/A

ALPHA TAURI RBPT

Debut:	2020 (Toro Rosso 2006-2019)
Races:	61
Pole Positions:	0
Victories:	1
Drivers Championships:	N/A
Constructors:	N/A

21. NYCK DE VRIES	**Netherlands**
DOB:	6/2/95
Debut:	2022
Races:	1
Pole Positions:	0
Podiums:	0
Victories:	0
Championships:	N/A

22. YUKI TSUNODA	**Japan**
DOB:	11/5/00
Debut:	2021
Races:	42
Pole Positions:	0
Podiums:	0
Victories:	0
Championships:	N/A

WILLIAMS MERCEDES

Debut:	1978
Races:	779
Pole Positions:	128
Victories:	114
Drivers Championships:	7
Constructors:	9

2. LOGAN SARGEANT — United States

DOB:	31/12/00
Debut:	2023
Races:	0
Pole Positions:	0
Podiums:	0
Victories:	0
Championships:	N/A

23. ALEXANDER ALBON — Thailand

DOB:	23/3/96
Debut:	2019
Races:	59
Pole Positions:	0
Podiums:	2
Victories:	0
Championships:	N/A

2023 CALENDAR

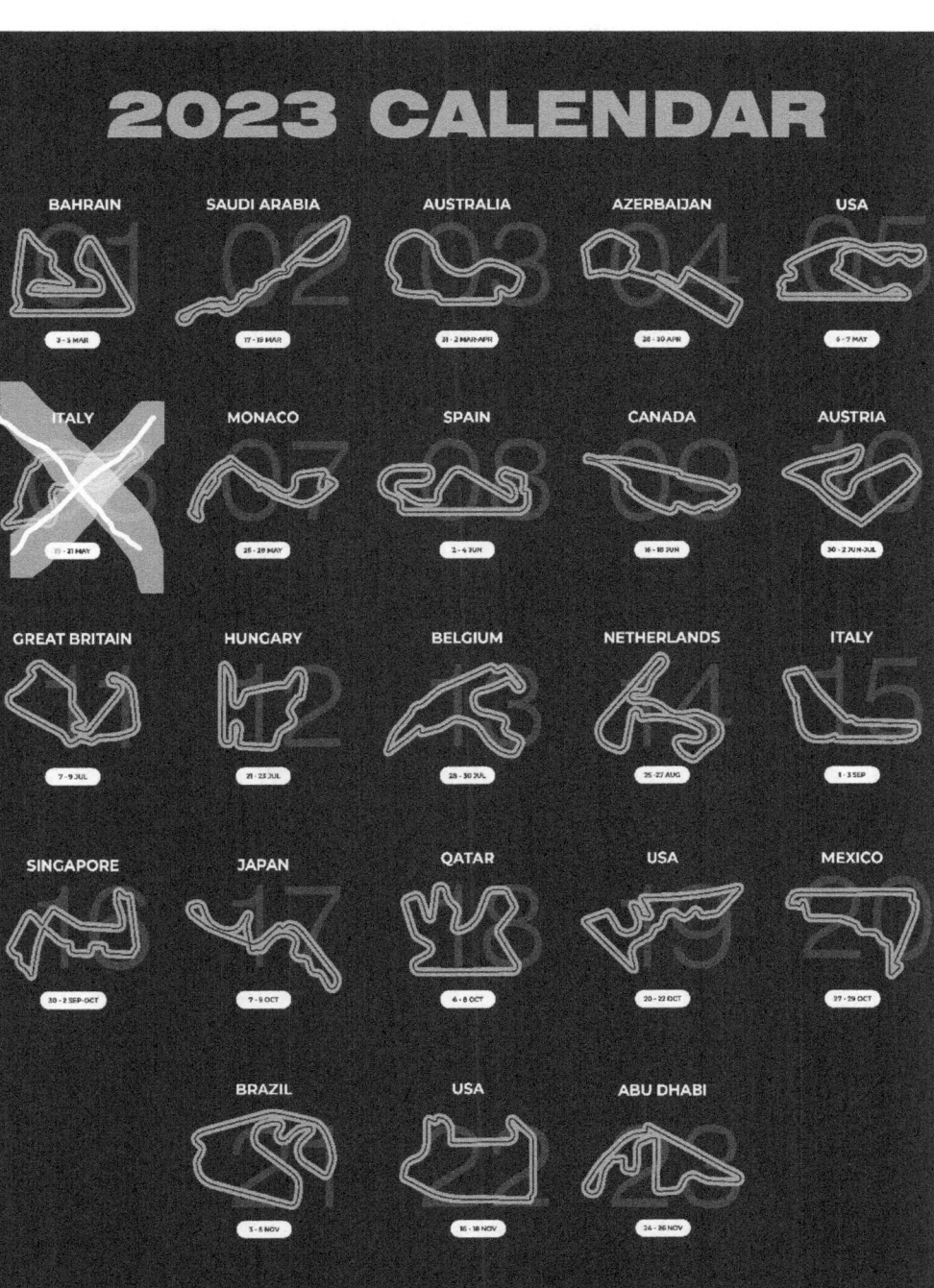

BAHRAIN — 3 - 5 MAR
SAUDI ARABIA — 17 - 19 MAR
AUSTRALIA — 31 - 2 MAR-APR
AZERBAIJAN — 28 - 30 APR
USA — 5 - 7 MAY

ITALY — 19 - 21 MAY
MONACO — 25 - 28 MAY
SPAIN — 2 - 4 JUN
CANADA — 16 - 18 JUN
AUSTRIA — 30 - 2 JUN-JUL

GREAT BRITAIN — 7 - 9 JUL
HUNGARY — 21 - 23 JUL
BELGIUM — 28 - 30 JUL
NETHERLANDS — 25 - 27 AUG
ITALY — 1 - 3 SEP

SINGAPORE — 30 - 2 SEP-OCT
JAPAN — 7 - 9 OCT
QATAR — 6 - 8 OCT
USA — 20 - 22 OCT
MEXICO — 27 - 29 OCT

BRAZIL — 3 - 5 NOV
USA — 16 - 18 NOV
ABU DHABI — 24 - 26 NOV

1. Sakhir, BAHRAIN

Scheduled Date:	March 5, 2023
Inaugural Event:	2004
Laps:	57
Lap Length:	5.412 km
Most victories:	Lewis Hamilton—5
	Ferrari - 7
2022 Winner:	Charles Leclerc
Lap Record:	Pedro de la Rosa—1:31:447 (2005)

Bahrain again hosts the opening event following the solitary three day pre-season test at the same venue a week earlier.

Charles Leclerc commenced Formula One's new era in 2022 with a commanding victory, followed home by team-mate, Carlos Sainz, for a Ferrari 1-2.

Lewis Hamilton rounded out the podium in a distant third after reigning champion, Max Verstappen, retired with several laps remaining, with the Dutchman joined by his Red Bull team-mate, Sergio Perez, on the final lap.

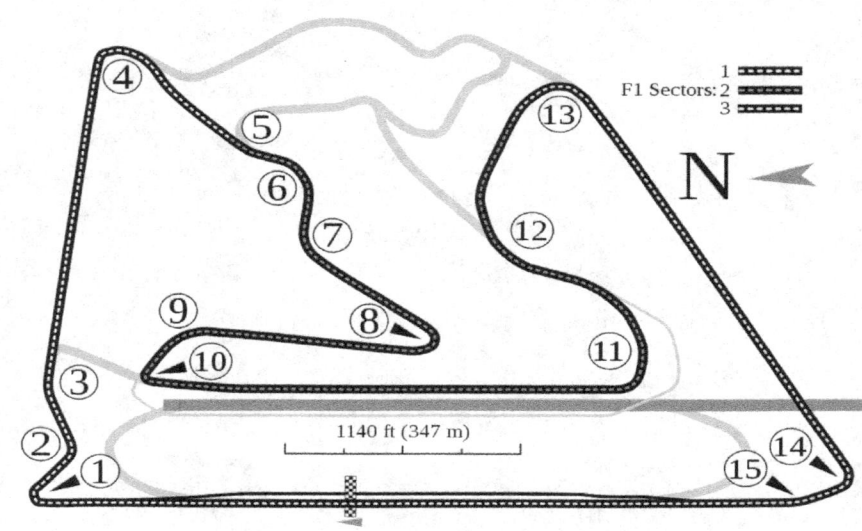

RACING

NOTES

2. Jeddah, SAUDI ARABIA

Scheduled Date:	March 19, 2023
Inaugural Event:	2021
Laps:	50
Lap Length:	6.175 km
Most victories:	Lewis Hamilton, Max Verstappen – 1
2022 Winner	Max Verstappen
Lap Record:	Lewis Hamilton – 1:30.734 (2021)

The inaugural event was acrimonious following multiple red flags triggered by the aggressive nature of the circuit. This culminated in a collision between championship protagonists, Max Verstappen and Lewis Hamilton, far from the first time in an unforgettable season, with the latter holding on for victory to draw level on points with the Dutchman heading to the title decider at Abu Dhabi. This race was watched by an estimated 1.445 million F1 fans.

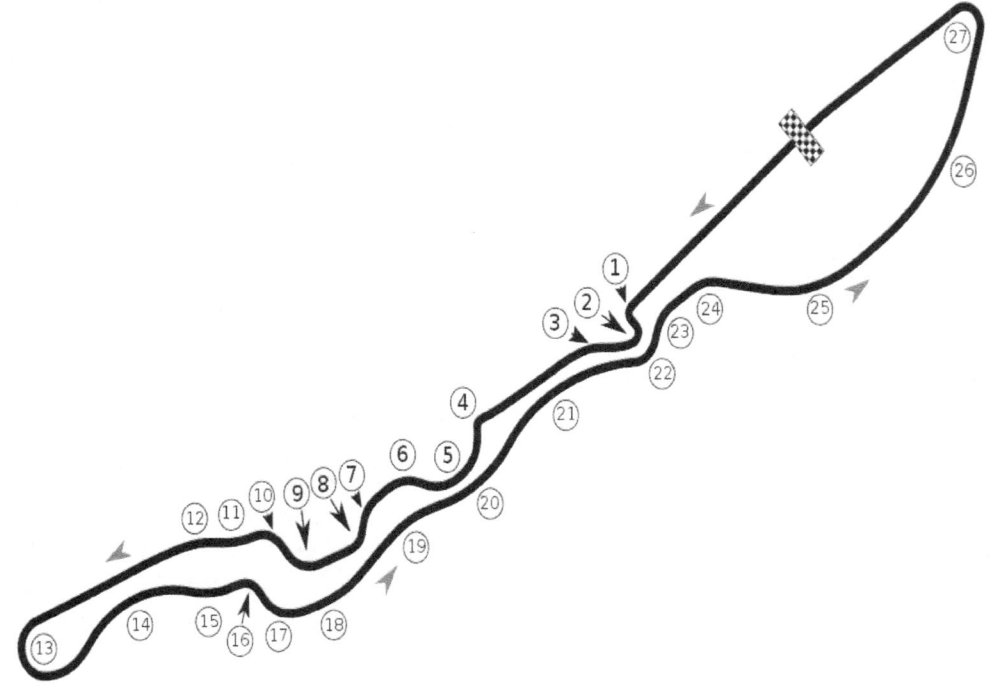

NOTES

3. Melbourne, AUSTRALIA

Date: April 2, 2023

Inaugural Event: 1996

Laps: 58

Lap Length: 5.279 km

Most victories: Michael Schumacher—4
Ferrari—8

2022 Winner: Charles Leclerc

Lap Record: Michael Schumacher —1:24.125 (2004)

Formula One returned to the longstanding curtain raiser in 2022 following a two year COVID induced absence, as the event proved more popular than ever with sell out figures, which has already been reached prior to this year's running.

With a contract through 2037 secured, alongside the addition of Formula 2 and 3 supporting categories across the weekend for the first time, and a new local hero to cheer on in Melbourne raised Oscar Piastri, the sport isn't leaving Australian shores anytime soon.

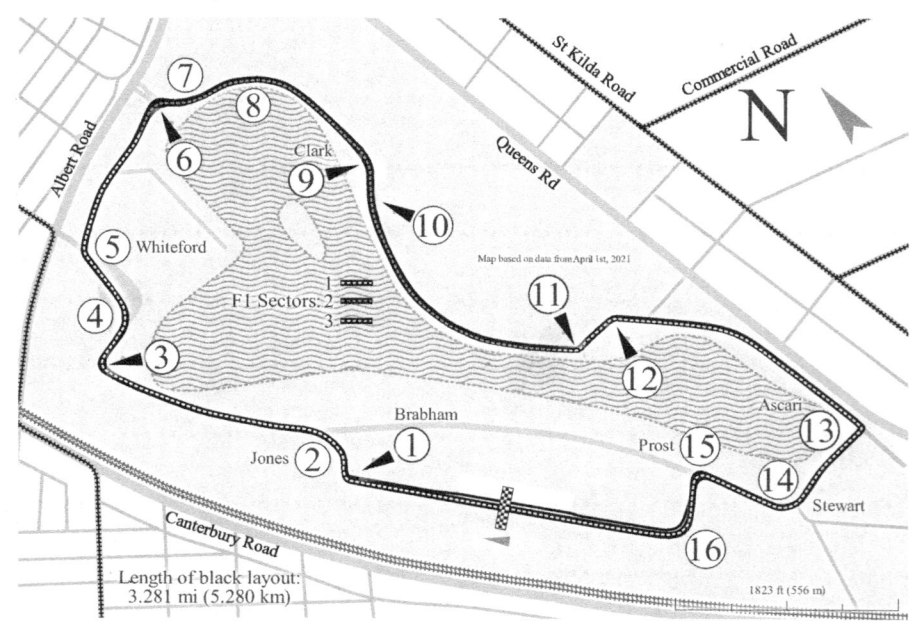

NOTES

4. Baku, AZERBAIJAN

Scheduled Date:	April 30, 2023
Inaugural Event:	2016
Laps:	51
Lap Length:	6.003 km
Most victories:	Nico Rosberg, Daniel Ricciardo, Lewis Hamilton, Valtteri Bottas, Sergio Perez, Max Verstappen —1
	Mercedes—3
2022 Winner:	Max Verstappen
Lap Record:	Charles Leclerc—1:43.009 (2019)

Following the strategic blundering which cost Charles Leclerc victory on home turf in Monaco, Ferrari's once fledgling campaign disintegrated spectacularly around the streets of Baku, as title rivals Red Bull again capitalised.

Leclerc's sixth pole position of the season came to nought, with the Monegasque joining Carlos Sainz, who retired with hydraulic issues on lap eight, on the sidelines following another power unit failure on lap twenty-one.

This left Max Verstappen and Sergio Perez to claim another 1-2, solidifying Red Bull's grasp on both championships. Mercedes' George Russell rounded out the podium, whilst team-mate, Lewis Hamilton, limped home in fourth, having battled crippling back issues inflicted by his porpoise prone W13 along the 2.2 km start/finish straight.

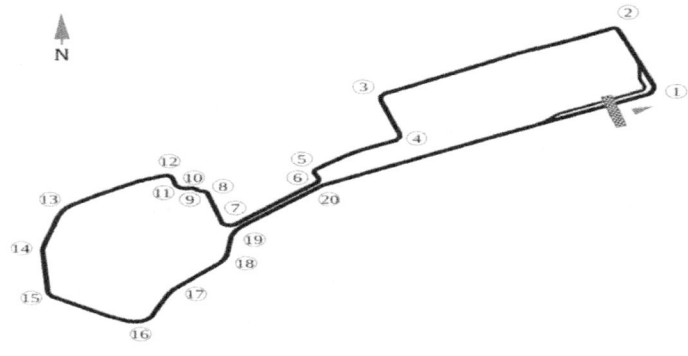

NOTES

5. Miami, UNITED STATES

Scheduled Date:	May 7, 2023
Inaugural Event:	2022
Laps:	57
Lap Length:	5.412 km
Most victories:	Max Verstappen – 1 (only edition)
2022 Winner:	Max Verstappen
Lap Record:	Max Verstappen – 1:16.361 (2022)

Formula One marked its' first visit to Florida in 2022, with the Miami Grand Prix becoming the most-watched event ever in the U.S. with an estimated 2.583 million viewers tuning in to watch Max Verstappen claiming the laurels from Charles Leclerc and Carlos Sainz.

Mick Schumacher made a costly late race error after colliding with close friend and mentor, Sebastian Vettel, which denied the German his first points haul.

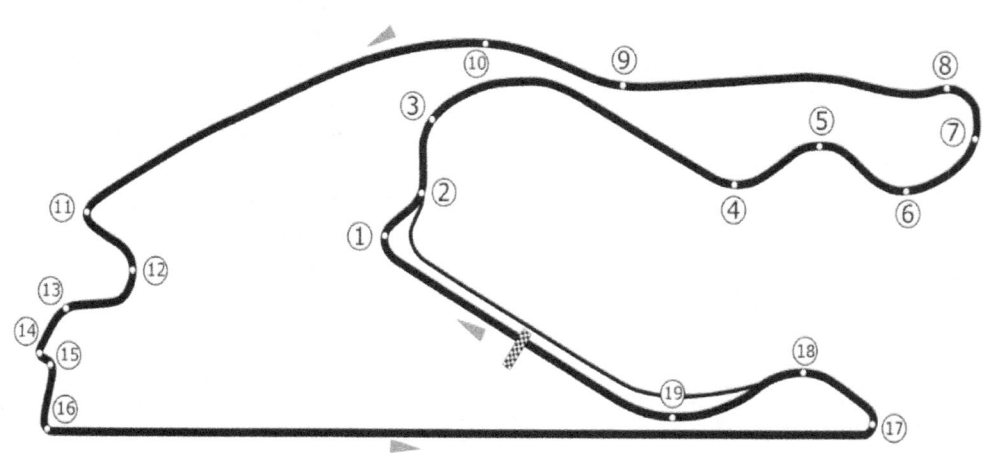

NOTES

....

....

....

....

....

....

....

....

....

....

....

....

....

6. Imola, EMILIA ROMAGNA

Scheduled Date:	May 21, 2023 **(CANCELLED)**
Inaugural Event:	1980
Laps:	63
Lap Length:	4.909 km
Most victories:	Michael Schumacher—7
	Williams, Ferrari—8
2022 Winner:	Max Verstappen
Lap Record:	Lewis Hamilton—1:15.484 (2020)

After multiple reliability induced retirements in the opening events, Max Verstappen claimed a much needed victory, headed home by team-mate, Sergio Perez, for Red Bull's first 1-2 since the 2016 Malaysian Grand Prix.

An unforced error from Charles Leclerc consigned the Monegasque to sixth and saw his early points' advantage eroded in a portent of what was to follow as the season developed.

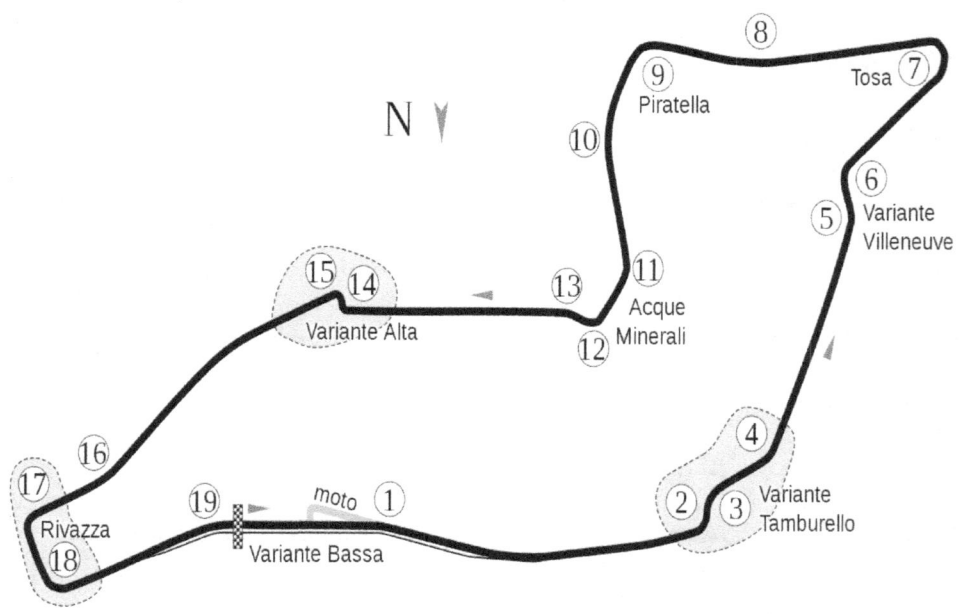

RACING
NOTES

....
....
....
....
....
....
....
....
....
....
....
....
....

7. Monaco, MONTE CARLO

Scheduled Date:	May 28, 2023
Inaugural Event:	1950
Laps:	78
Lap Length:	3.337 km
Most victories:	Ayrton Senna—6
	McLaren—15
2022 Winner:	Sergio Perez
Lap Record:	Lewis Hamilton —1:12.909 (2021)

Charles Leclerc's repeated his 2021 pole position heroics in front of his compatriots, and this time the Monegasque was able to take to the grid.

However, following a heavily delayed start due to rain, strategic blundering would cost Leclerc a famous victory.

Mick Schumacher triggered a red flag following a crash at the Swimming Pool on lap 24. Sergio Perez was the Red Bull beneficiary on this occasion, leading home Carlos Sainz and team-mate, Max Verstappen.

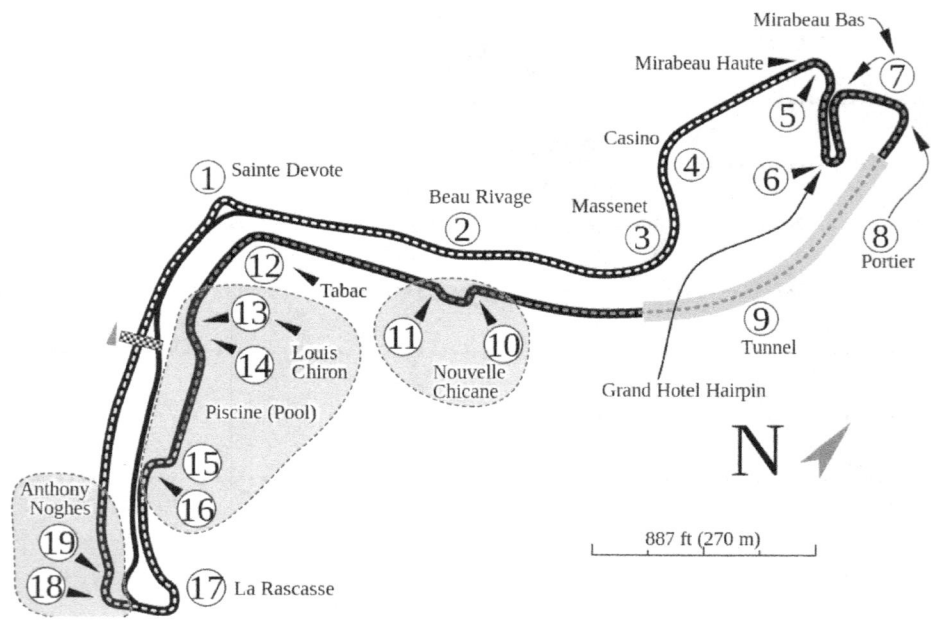

NOTES

8. Barcelona, SPAIN

Scheduled Date:	June 4, 2023
Inaugural Event:	1991
Laps:	66
Lap Length:	4.675 km
Most victories:	Michael Schumacher, Lewis Hamilton – 6
	Ferrari—8
2022 Winner:	Max Verstappen
Lap Record:	Max Verstappen—1:18.149 (2021)

Charles Leclerc appeared destined for victory having built an early lead from pole position, only for power unit failure – not for the final occasion across the season, to curtail his charge.

Max Verstappen capitalised for an unlikely triumph after battling DRS issues and traffic earlier in the race, leading home team-mate, Sergio Perez, who felt he should have been provided the opportunity to fight for victory.

Formula One will go back to the future in 2023, following the restoration of the final corner utilised prior to 2007, signalling the demise of the derided right, left, right hand chicane which greatly slowed cars entry on the run into the start/finish straight.

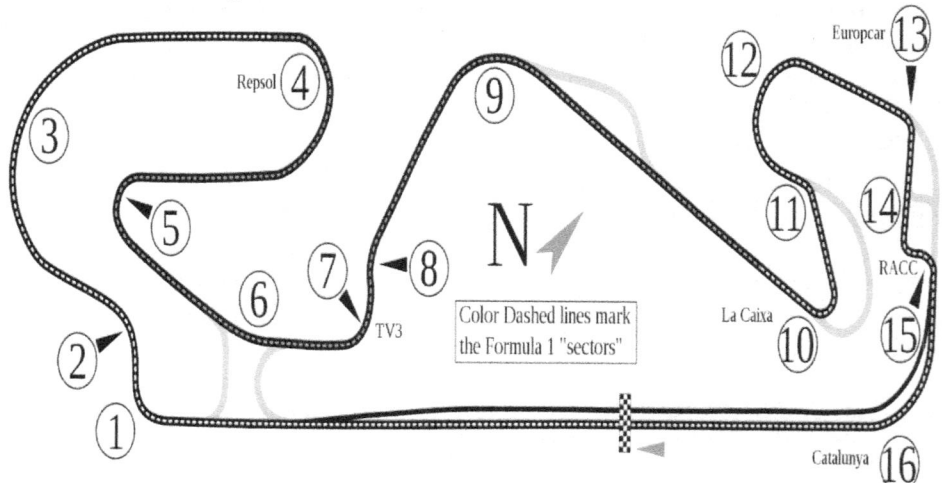

RACING

NOTES

....

....

....

....

....

....

....

....

....

....

....

....

....

9. Montreal, CANADA

Scheduled Date:	June 18, 2023
Inaugural Event:	1978
Laps:	70
Lap Length:	4.361 km
Most victories:	Michael Schumacher,
	Lewis Hamilton— 7
	Ferrari—11
2022 Winner:	Max Verstappen
Lap Record:	Valtteri Bottas —1:13.078 (2019)

The cosmopolitan Montreal returned to the calendar following its' pandemic induced absence in 2022, with the popular Notre Dame Island situated circuit renowned for producing quality racing.

Following a wet qualifying, Max Verstappen held off a charging Carlos Sainz for victory, as Red Bull asserted its' authority on the title fight.

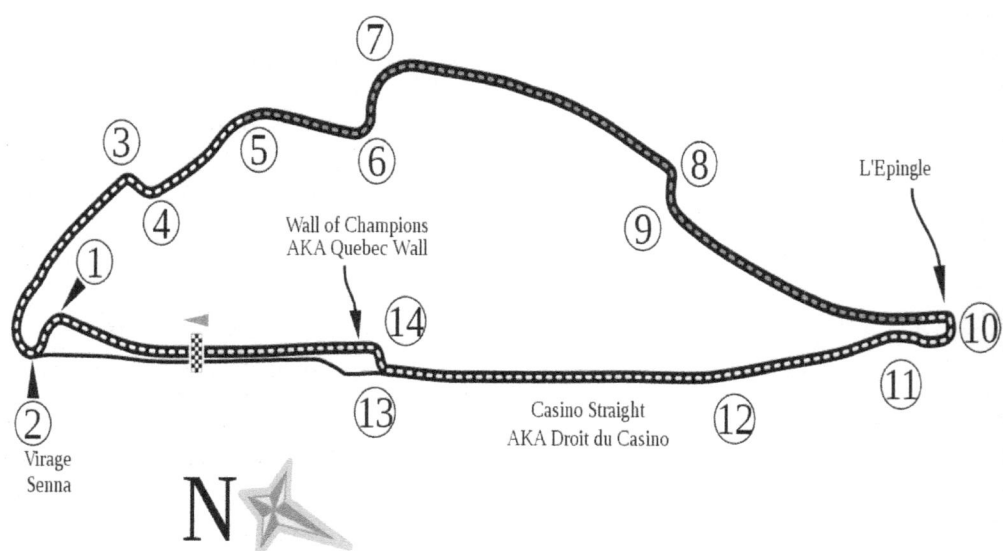

RACING

NOTES

10. Spielberg, AUSTRIA

Scheduled Date:	July 2, 2023
Inaugural Event:	1970
Laps:	71
Lap Length:	4.318 km
Most victories:	Alain Prost—3
	McLaren, Ferrari—6
2022 Winner	Charles Leclerc
Lap Record:	Carlos Sainz —1:05.619 (2020)

Charles Leclerc held his nerve for a much needed victory from Max Verstappen, following a frustrating run of reliability and strategic blunders. Team-mate, Carlos Sainz, fresh off his maiden victory, wasn't as fortunate, with the Spaniard's power unit expiring in the closing stages.

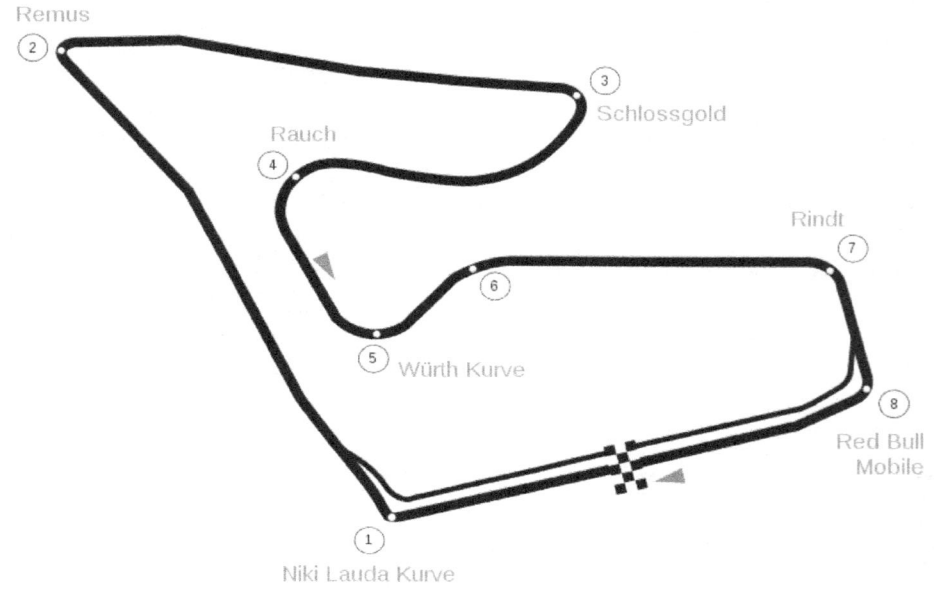

NOTES

....
....
....
....
....
....
....
....
....
....
....
....
....

11. Silverstone, GREAT BRITAIN

Scheduled Date:	July 9, 2023
Inaugural Event:	1950
Laps:	52
Lap Length:	5.891 km
Most victories:	Lewis Hamilton—8
	Ferrari—13
2022 Winner:	Carlos Sainz
Lap Record:	Max Verstappen —1:27.097 (2020)

The parochial British crowd always make this event one of the most memorable on the calendar.

Carlos Sainz claimed his maiden victory in 2022 after another of Ferrari's fickle strategic calls hindered team-mate Charles Leclerc's prospects.

The breakthrough was overshadowed by Zhou Guanyu's frightening opening lap crash, with the Chinese's Alfa Romeo launched upside down into the turn one runoff before skidding into the catch fencing metres away from spectators, though he mercifully emerged unscathed following a precarious rescue effort.

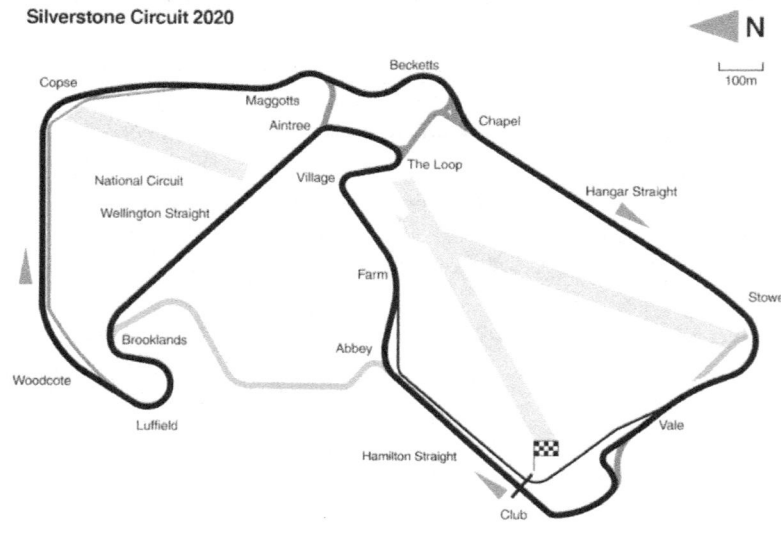

Silverstone Circuit 2020

RACING

NOTES

12. Budapest, HUNGARY

Scheduled Date:	July 23, 2023
Inaugural Event:	1986
Laps:	70
Lap Length:	4.381 km
Most victories:	Lewis Hamilton—8
	McLaren—11
2022 Winner:	Max Verstappen
Lap Record:	Lewis Hamilton —1:16:627 (2020)

Max Verstappen overcame power unit issues in qualifying to charge from tenth on the grid to a commanding victory, followed home by the Mercedes duo of Lewis Hamilton and George Russell.

Ferrari's strategy again came under the spotlight after Charles Leclerc's flagging championship aspirations were further dented, with the Monegasque consigned to sixth after being placed on the slower hard tyre compound.

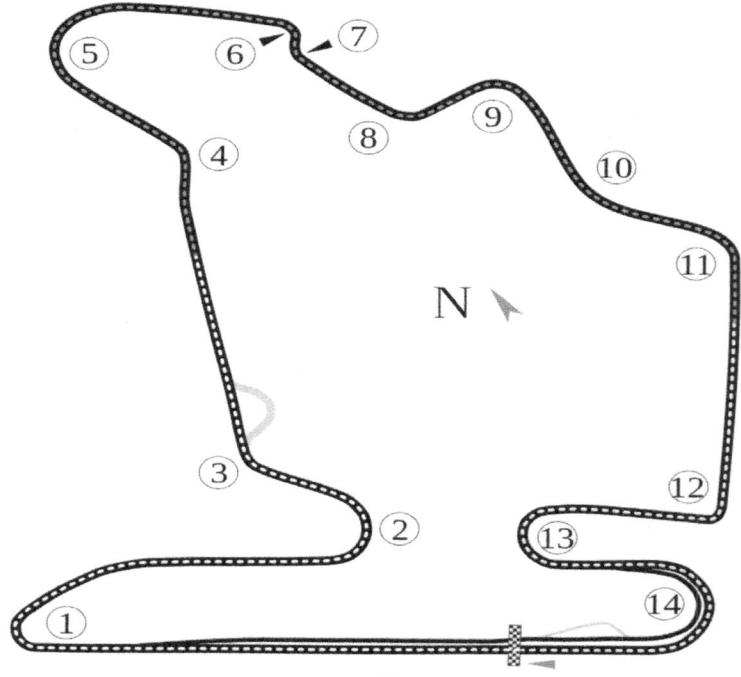

RACING

NOTES

13. Stavelot, BELGIUM

Scheduled Date:	July 30, 2023
Inaugural Event:	1950
Laps:	44
Lap Length:	7.004 km
Most victories:	Michael Schumacher—6
	Ferrari—13
2021 Winner:	Max Verstappen
Lap Record:	Valtteri Bottas —1:46.286 (2018)

The famed Stavelot circuit features much earlier on the calendar than its' customary post mid-season break slot, this time sending F1 into its' European summer siesta.

Max Verstappen lined up fourteenth in 2022 despite qualifying fastest owing to exceeding his power unit quota, though the Dutchman benefitted from several other drivers meeting the same fate, leading to an unrecognisable grid from the order on Saturday.

Verstappen climbed into the lead by lap 12 and was never headed, as team-mate, Sergio Perez, followed him home for a Red Bull 1-2, as Charles Leclerc's remote title prospects took yet another blow after incurring a pit lane speeding time penalty which dropped him to sixth.

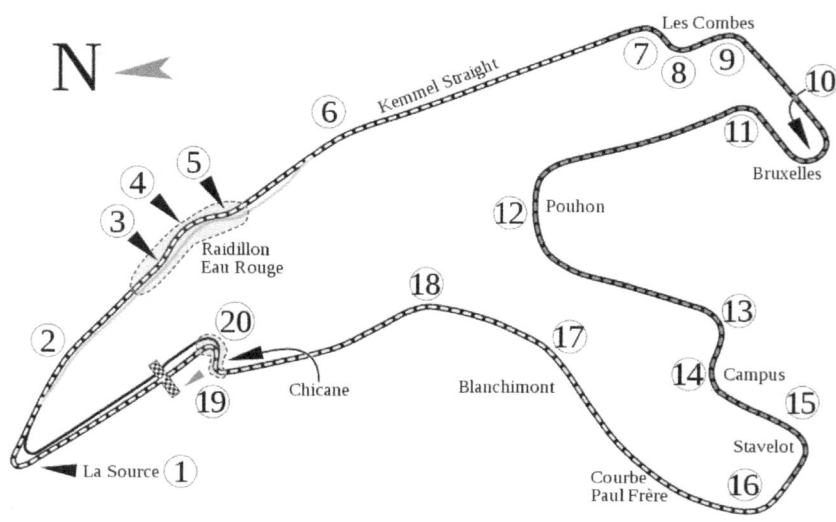

NOTES

14. North Holland, NETHERLANDS

Scheduled Date:	August 27, 2023
Inaugural Event:	1952
Laps:	72
Lap Length:	4.259 km
Most victories:	Jim Clark—4
	Ferrari—9
2021 Winner:	Max Verstappen
Lap Record:	Lewis Hamilton —1:11.097 (2021)

Zandvoort belatedly returned to the calendar in 2021 for the first time since 1985, having been denied its intended return twelve months earlier due to the pandemic, as Max Verstappen claimed a hugely popular victory in front of his compatriots. The sea of Dutch orange along the main straight leading into 'Tarzan', accompanied by the 'Super Max' tune dedicated to Verstappen, provided an electric atmosphere.

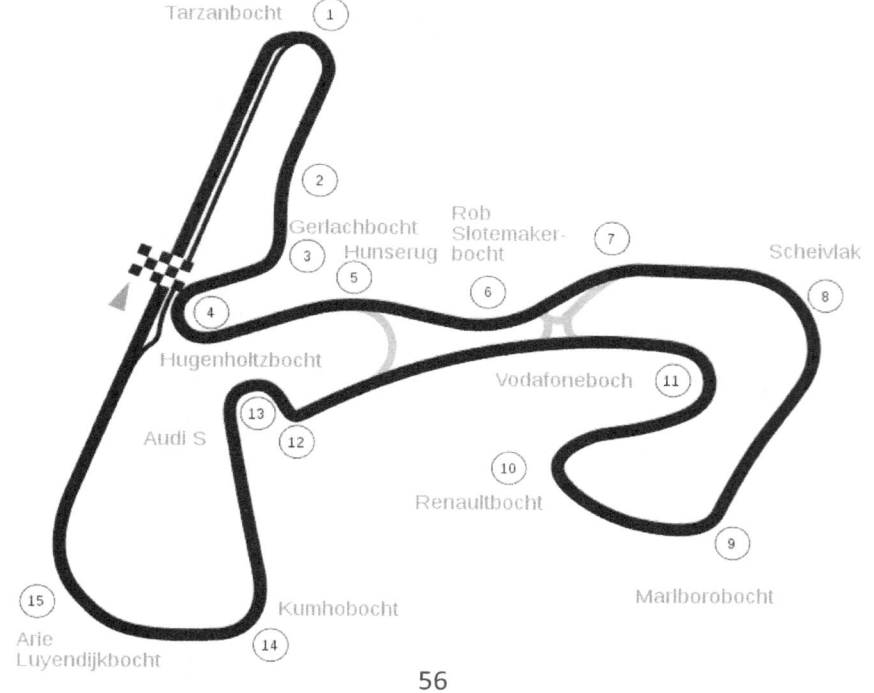

RACING

NOTES

15. Monza, ITALY

Scheduled Date: September 3, 2023

Inaugural Event: 1950

Laps: 53

Lap Length: 5.793 km

Most victories: Michael Schumacher, Lewis Hamilton—5

Ferrari—20

2022 Winner: Max Verstappen

Lap Record: Rubens Barrichello —1:21.046 (2004)

Charles Leclerc was unable to deliver a popular Ferrari victory from pole position, with Max Verstappen claiming his fifth consecutive victory. A late race fight between the pair was denied by the safety car, triggered by 2021 victor Daniel Ricciardo.

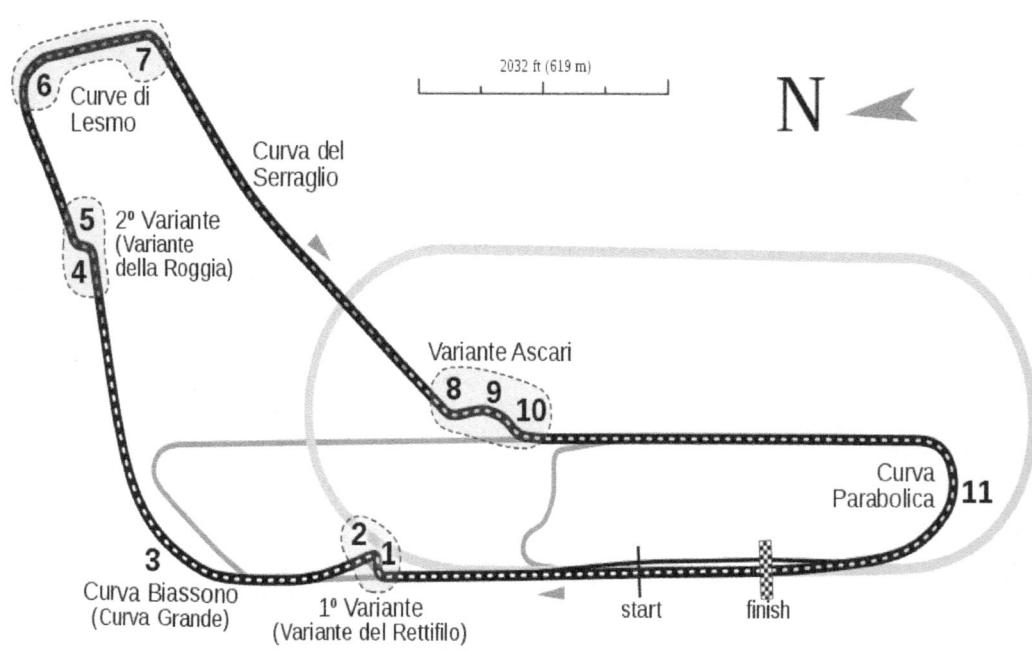

NOTES

....

....

....

....

....

....

....

....

....

....

....

....

....

16. Marina Bay, SINGAPORE

Scheduled Date:	September 17, 2023
Inaugural Event:	2008
Laps:	63
Lap Length:	4.928 km
Most Victories:	Sebastian Vettel—5
	Mercedes—4
2022 Winner:	Sergio Perez
Lap Record:	N/A (revised circuit layout from 2023)

The scene for Formula One's first night race returned to the calendar in 2022 and has undergone a transformation ahead of the 2023 event, following the removal of the former turn 16-19 complex which will lead to significantly faster times.

Sergio Perez prevailed in 2022 following a delayed start due to heavy downpour after surviving the imposition of a five second post-race time penalty for falling too far behind the safety car to claim his second victory for the season.

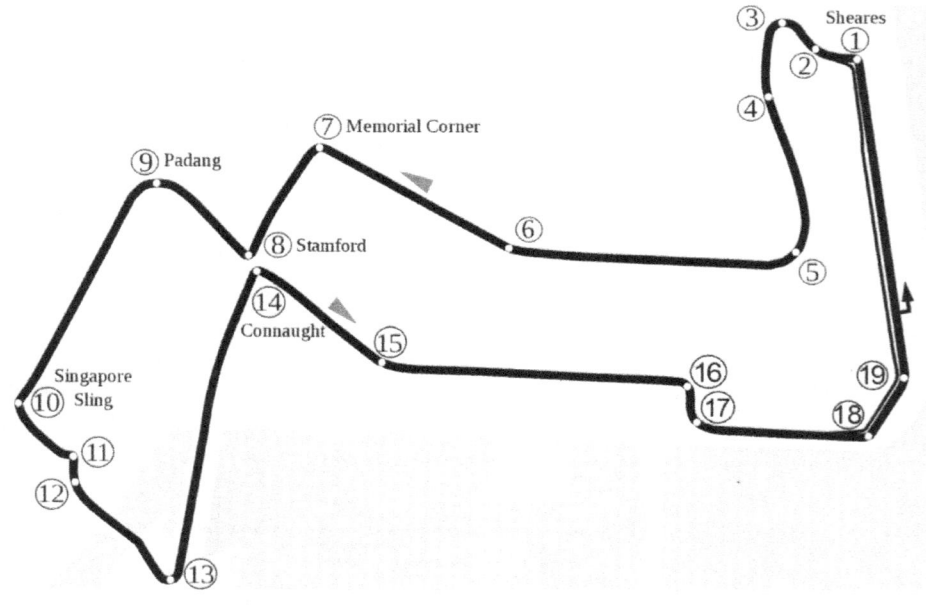

RACING

NOTES

....

....

....

....

....

....

....

....

....

....

....

....

....

17. Suzuka, JAPAN

Scheduled Date:	September 24, 2023
Inaugural Event:	1987
Laps:	53
Lap Length:	5.807 km
Most victories:	Michael Schumacher—6
	McLaren, Ferrari—7
2021 Winner:	Max Verstappen
Lap Record:	Lewis Hamilton —1:30.983 (2019)

Formula One's recent reluctance to race in wet conditions threatened to spoil the chances of the iconic Japanese circuit from staging its' first event since 2019.

Once running finally commenced, little over half distance of 28 laps were possible within the time limit. That was all Max Verstappen required to secure his second consecutive title in anti-climactic circumstances, with confusion over the points awarded over the reduced distance.

The Dutchman was only ensured of the crown once it was established that the full quota of points could be awarded following much deliberation over the regulations, which had been updated in the wake of the 2021 Belgian GP fiasco.

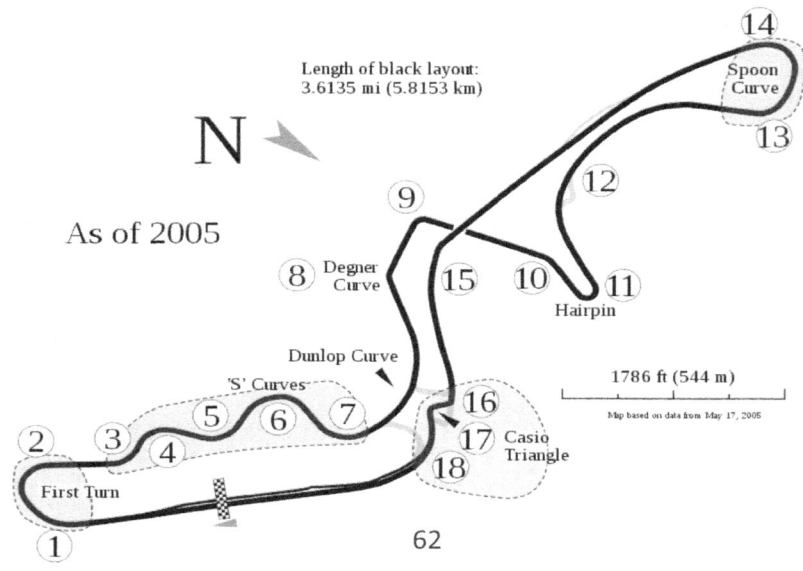

RACING

NOTES

18. Losail, QATAR

Scheduled Date: October 8, 2023

Inaugural Event: 2021

Laps: 57

Lap Length: 5.380 km

Most victories: Lewis Hamilton—1

                                 Mercedes—1

2021 Winner   Lewis Hamilton

                                 (no event in 2022 due to FIFA World Cup)

Lap Record: Max Verstappen—1:23.196 (2021)

Having staged its' inaugural event in 2021 as a replacement for Australia due to the pandemic, Qatar returns to the calendar on a permanent basis following a twelve month absence to cater for the FIFA World Cup.

Lewis Hamilton claimed a decisive victory on that occasion, followed home by Max Verstappen who retained a slender points lead with two races remaining, whilst Fernando Alonso claimed his first podium since returning to the sport at the start of the season for Alpine, and the double World Champion's first in the sport altogether since 2014.

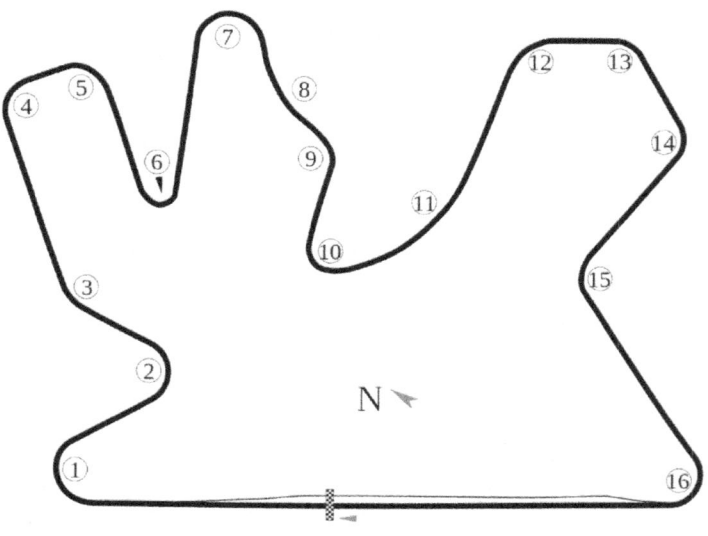

NOTES

19. Austin (Texas), UNITED STATES

Scheduled Date:	October 22, 2023
Inaugural Event:	2012
Laps:	56
Lap Length:	5.513 km
Most victories:	Lewis Hamilton—6
	Mercedes—5
2022 Winner:	Max Verstappen
Lap Record:	Charles Leclerc —1:36.169 (2019)

Having secured the drivers' championship in Japan with Max Verstappen, Red Bull wrapped up its' first constructors' title since 2013 at Austin, after the Dutchman led Lewis Hamilton home.

A scary collision between future Aston Martin team-mates, Lance Stroll and Fernando Alonso, which saw the latter speared airborne perilously close towards the Armco barriers, didn't prevent the Spaniard from recovering to finish seventh.

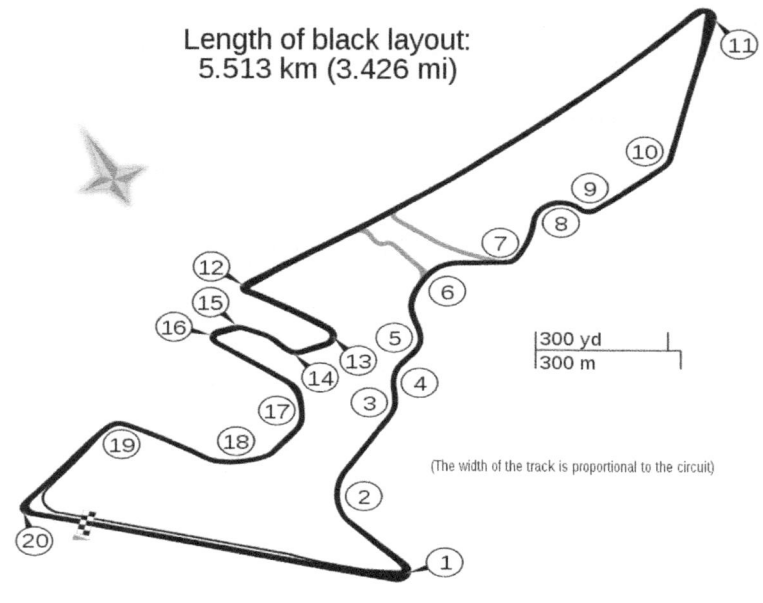

Length of black layout:
5.513 km (3.426 mi)

300 yd
300 m

(The width of the track is proportional to the circuit)

RACING

NOTES

....

....

....

....

....

....

....

....

....

....

....

....

....

20. Mexico City, MEXICO

Scheduled Date:	October 29, 2023
Inaugural Event:	1963
Laps:	71
Lap Length:	4.304 km
Most victories:	Max Verstappen—3
	Williams, Mercedes, Red Bull —3
2022 Winner:	Max Verstappen
Lap Record:	Valtteri Bottas —1:17.774 (2021)

Max Verstappen made it eight wins from the past nine races with his fourth victory in Mexico, which moved the Dutchman clear of Jim Clark's longstanding record.

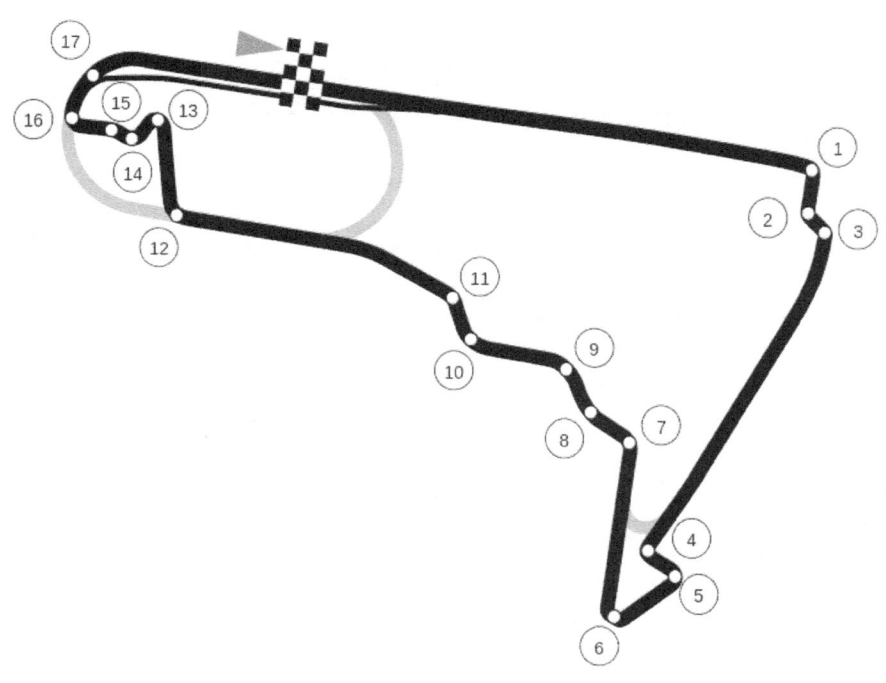

RACING

NOTES

21. Sao Paulo, BRAZIL

Scheduled Date:	November 5, 2023
Inaugural Event:	1973
Laps:	71
Lap Length:	4.309 km
Most victories:	Michael Schumacher—4
	Ferrari—9
2022 Winner:	George Russell
Lap Record:	Valtteri Bottas —1:10.540 (2018)

With an estimated 1.4 million viewers, Mercedes broke through to record its first and only win of the season after eight consecutive campaigns with no less than nine, as George Russell claimed his maiden victory, followed home by team-mate, Lewis Hamilton.

Kevin Magnussen provided the other highlight of the weekend after registering his and Haas' first pole position on Friday prior to the Saturday sprint race. The Dane's euphoria was short lived following an opening lap retirement in Sunday's race proper.

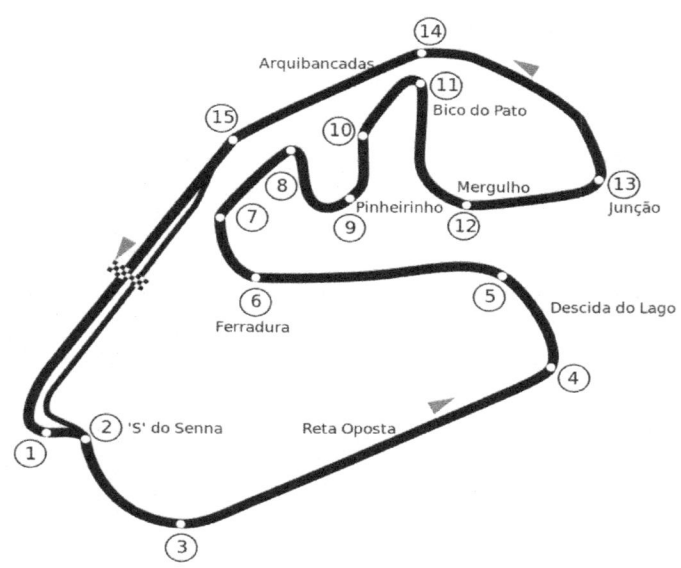

NOTES

....

....

....

....

....

....

....

....

....

....

....

....

22. Nevada, LAS VEGAS

Scheduled Date:	November 18, 2023
Inaugural Event:	2023
Laps:	50
Lap Length:	6.120 km
Most victories:	N/A
2022 Winner:	N/A
Lap Record:	N/A

The sport visits its' second new (or returning in this case) American venue in as many seasons for the penultimate stop on the calendar, under the high rolling Vegas lights.

Having last hosted an event in 1982 under the exotic Caesar's Palace moniker, the race will be uniquely staged on Saturday evening, leading to rare Sunday afternoon viewing in the southern hemisphere instead of the standard early Monday morning routine for races throughout the Americas.

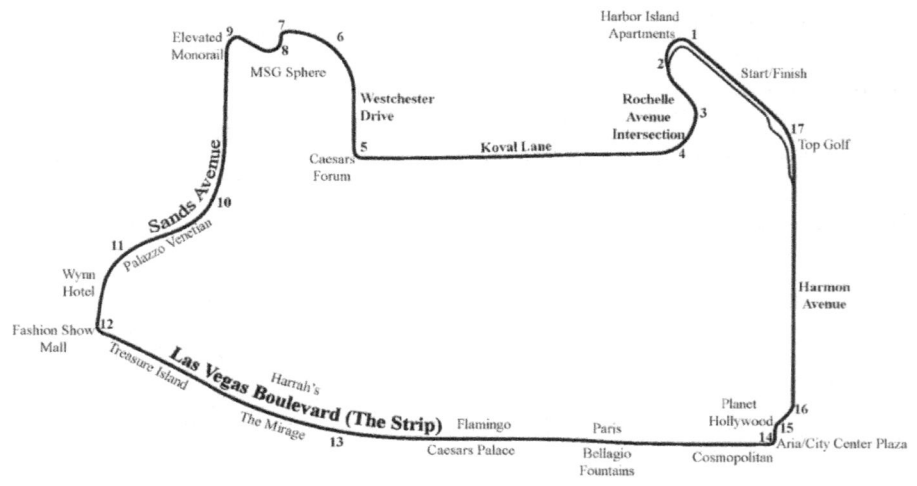

RACING
NOTES

....

....

....

....

....

....

....

....

....

....

....

....

23. Yas Marina, ABU DHABI

Scheduled Date:	November 26, 2023
Inaugural Event:	2009
Laps:	55
Lap Length:	5.554 km
Most victories:	Lewis Hamilton—5
	Mercedes—6
2022 Winner	Max Verstappen
Lap Record:	Max Verstappen—1:26.103 (2021)

The season finale lacked the acrimony witnessed a year prior, as Max Verstappen coronated his second crown with an unprecedented fifteenth victory of the season, though it was another former Red Bull champion, Sebastian Vettel, who enjoyed the limelight in the four-time champ's swansong, with the German crossing the chequered flag in tenth.

Despite this and team-mate Lance Stroll's eighth place, the points' haul was insufficient for Aston Martin to overcome Alfa Romeo for sixth in the constructors' standings on best result countback.

Charles Leclerc secured second in the drivers' standings from Sergio Perez after holding off the Mexican for the same race position, though it was scant consolation for the Monegasque, who harboured title aspirations following two victories from the opening three events.

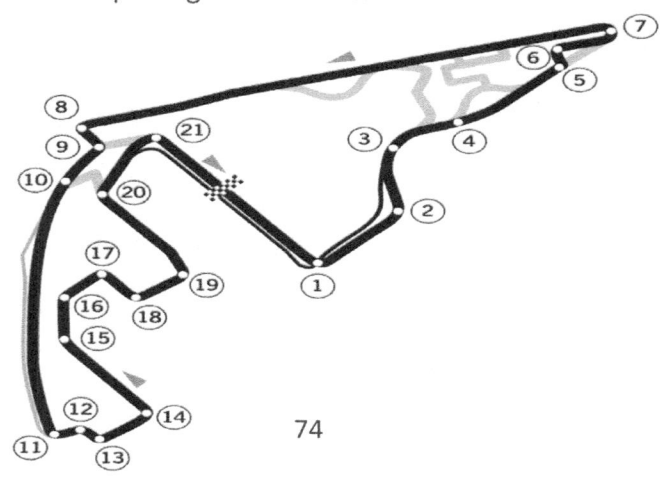

74

RACING

NOTES

....

....

....

....

....

....

....

....

....

....

....

....

....

RACING

NOTES

NOTES

RACING

NOTES

NOTES

....

....

....

....

....

....

....

....

....

....

....

....

....

RACING

NOTES

....

....

....

....

....

....

....

....

....

....

....

....

....

RACING
NOTES

··
··
··
··
··
··
··
··
··
··
··
··
··

RACING
NOTES

RACING

NOTES

NOTES

NOTES

RACING

NOTES

....
....
....
....
....
....
....
....
....
....
....
....
....

RACING

NOTES

NOTES

RACING

NOTES

NOTES

NOTES

RACING
NOTES

RACING
NOTES

NOTES

RACING
NOTES

NOTES

NOTES

RACING

NOTES

....

....

....

....

....

....

....

....

....

....

....

....

....

RACING

NOTES

....

....

....

....

....

....

....

....

....

....

....

....

....

RACING
NOTES

···

···

···

···

···

···

···

···

···

···

···

···

···

RACING

NOTES

RACING
NOTES

··

··

··

··

··

··

··

··

··

··

··

··

··

AUTOgraphs

AUTOgraphs

AUTOgraphs

AUTOgraphs

AUTOgraphs

AUTOgraphs

AUTOgraphs

AUTOgraphs

AUTOgraphs

AUTOgraphs

AUTOgraphs

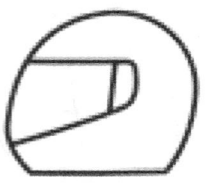

AUTOgraphs

AUTOgraphs

AUTOgraphs

AUTOgraphs

AUTOgraphs

AUTOgraphs

AUTOgraphs

AUTOgraphs

AUTOgraphs

AUTOgraphs

AUTOgraphs

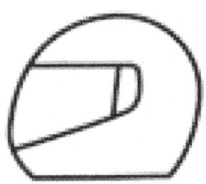

AUTOgraphs

AUTOgraphs

AUTOgraphs

AUTOgraphs

AUTOgraphs

AUTOgraphs

REFERENCES

AEPA Racing. (2021). *File:Albert Park Circuit 2021.svg*. [Own work]. Retrieved 02/14/23 in Wikipedia. https://upload.wikimedia.org/wikipedia/commons/archive/3/31/202104032 04531%21Albert_Lake_Park_Street_Circuit_in_Melbourne%2C_Australia.svg.

Antoine266. (2020). *Silverstone Circuit 2020*. Great Britain. [Own work]. In Wikipedia. https://commons.wikimedia.org/w/index.php?curid=97517203.

Arz. (2008). *Circuit Yas-Island*. Abu Dhabi. [Own work]. In Wikipedia. https://commons.wikimedia.org/w/index.php?curid=4394985.

Bbb2007. (2018). *Circuit Paul Ricard 2018 layout map*. France. [Own work]. In Wikipedia. https://commons.wikimedia.org/w/index.php?curid=67412820.

Ch1902. (2008). *Circuit Interlagos* Formula1.com map. Sao Paulo. [Own work]. In Wikipedia. https://commons.wikimedia.org/wiki/File:Circuit_Interlagos.svg.

Cobb, H. & Boxall-Legge. (2023). *Everything We Know About F1 2023: Drivers, Cars, Tracks & More*. [Article]. Motorsport.com. Retrieved 02/18/23 from https://au.motorsport.com/f1/news/2023-f1-season-everything-we-know-drivers-cars-tracks-more/10401362/.

Coch, M. (2022*). Focus on Sidepod Design for F1 2023 Development*. [Article]. Speedcafe.com. Retrieved 09/26/22 from https://www.speedcafe.com/2022/09/26/focus-on-sidepod-design-for-f1-2023-development/.

Cooper, A. (2023). *Why Alfa Romeo Has Kept It's Blade Roll Hoop on 2023 F1 Car*. [Article]. Motorsport.com. Retrieved 02/07/23 from https://au.motorsport.com/f1/news/why-alfa-romeo-has-kept-its-blade-roll-hoop-on-2023-f1-car/10429037/#:~:text=For%202023%20the%20FIA%20duly,new%20physical%20homologation%20test%20where.

Dromara. (2023*). Race Tracks, Circuit for Motorsport and Autosport. Calendar Season 2023*. [Vector Image]. Shutterstock. Retrieved from https://www.shutterstock.com/image-vector/race-tracks-circuit-motorsport-auto-sport-2248444161.

Federation Internationale de l'Automobile. (2022). *2023 Formula 1 Technical Regulations.* [PDF]. FIA. Retrieved from https://www.fia.com/sites/default/files/fia_2023_formula_1_technical_regulations_-_issue_4_-_2022-12-07.pdf.

Formula One World Championship Limited. (2023). *F1 Glossary: Definition of CFD.* [Webpage]. Formula1.com. Retrieved from https://www.formula1.com/en/championship/inside-f1/glossary.html#:~:text=CFD,with%20traditional%20wind%20tunnel%20research.

Foster, M. (2022). *Porpoising in F1: What is it and how harmful is it to driver health?* [Article]. Planetsport. Retrieved 02/14/23 from https://www.planetsport.com/motorsport/news/porpoising-in-f1-what-is-it-and-how-harmful-to-driver-health.

GabrielStella. (2021). *Jeddah Street Circuit 2021.* Saudi Arabia. [Own work]. In Wikipedia. https://commons.wikimedia.org/w/index.php?curid=101760446.

(2021). *Hard Rock Stadium Circuit, Miami.* [Own work]. In Wikipedia, https://commons.wikimedia.org/wiki/File:Hard_Rock_Stadium_Circuit_2022.svg.

Girardelli, G. (2014). *Austin Circuit.* United States. [Own work]. In Wikipedia. https://commons.wikimedia.org/w/index.php?curid=36176519.

Guymer, C. (2023). *Artistic Parody Interpretation of Jay Hirano Photography's 2022 SUZUKA, JAPAN, 09.10.2022; #1, Max VERSTAPPEN, NDL, Oracle Red Bull Racing RB18 Honda ahead of #16, Charles LECLERC, MCO, Team Scuderia Ferrari, F1-75, Ferrari 065 engine during the F1 Grand Prix.* [Own work].

(2023). *Artistic Caricature Parody of Charles LeClerc.* [Own work].

(2023). *Artistic Caricature Parody of Lando Norris.* [Own work].

(2023). *Artistic Caricature Parody of Lewis Hamilton.* [Own work].

(2023). *Artistic Caricature Parody of Max Verstappen.* [Own work].

(2023). *Artistic Caricature Parody of Nico Hulkenberg.* [Own work].

(2023). *Artistic Caricature Parody of Pierre Gasley.* [Own work].

[2023]. *Artistic Caricature Parody of Zhou Ganyou.* [Own work].

Hazim Fikri, A. (2022). *File:Planned 2023 Marina Bay Street Circuit Layout.png* [Own work]. In Wikipedia. Retrieved from https://commons.wikimedia.org/wiki/File:Planned_2023_Marina_Bay_Street_Circuit_layout.png.

Hmdwgf (2022). *Las Vegas Street Circuit.* [Own work]. In Wikipedia. Retrieved from https://commons.wikimedia.org/wiki/File:Las_Vegas_street_circuit.png.

Holiday, M. (2022). *What are the Different Coloured Tyres in F1?* [Article]. Formula Nerds. Retrieved 12/26/22 from https://www.formulanerds.com/explainer/what-are-the-different-coloured-tyres-in-f1/#:~:text=The%20soft%20tyre%20is%20always,the%20full%20wet%20being%20blue.

Homologation (motorsport). (n.d.). In Wikipedia. Retrieved from https://en.wikipedia.org/wiki/Homologation_(motorsport).

Inspired Images / 1105 Images. (2021). *Racing_Flags_Race_Chequered_RacingFlag_Formula.* [Vector Image]. Pixabay. Retrieved from https://pixabay.com/illustrations/racing-flags-race-checkered-1312447.

Jay Hirano Photography. (2022). *SUZUKA, JAPAN, 09.10.2022; #1, Max VERSTAPPEN, NDL, Oracle Red Bull Racing RB18 Honda ahead of #16, Charles LECLERC, MCO, Team Scuderia Ferrari, F1-75, Ferrari 065 engine during the F1 Grand Prix.* [Cover Image Photo]. Shutterstock. Retrieved from https://www.shutterstock.com/image-photo/suzuka-japan-0910-1-max-verstappen-2214931801.

Mitchell, R. (2022). *Pirelli Adds New Tyre Compound to F1 for 2023.* [Article]. Racing News 365. Retrieved 11/23/22 from https://racingnews365.com/pirelli-adds-new-tyre-compound-to-f1-for-2023.

MotorOilStains. (2016). *Baku-F1-Street-Circuit-rev1.* Azerbaijan. [Own work] in Wikipedia. https://commons.wikimedia.org/w/index.php?curid=47984339.

Noble, J. (2023). *Why Ferrari Can Run the Front Wing Design that Mercedes Could Not.* [Article]. Motorsport.com. Retrieved 02/14/23 from https://au.motorsport.com/f1/news/why-ferrari-can-run-the-front-wing-design-that-mercedes-could-not/10432016/.

Paleski, Y. (2022). *Colorful Illustration with Pit Stop Workers and Engineers*. [Vector Image]. Shutterstock. Retrieved from https://www.shutterstock.com/image-vector/colorful-illustration-pit-stop-workers-engineers-328955624.

Parc Fermé. *(n.d.)*. In Wikipedia. Retrieved from https://en.wikipedia.org/wiki/Parc_ferm%C3%A9.

Pitlane02. (2011). *Circuit Red Bull Ring*. Austria [Own work]. In Wikipedia. Retrieved from https://commons.wikimedia.org/w/index.php?curid=16743759.

(2011*). Circuit Red Bull Ring*. Styria. [Own work]. In Wikipedia. Retrieved from https://commons.wikimedia.org/w/index.php?curid=16743759.

(2012). *Circuit Park Zandvoort-1999*. Netherlands. [Own work] In Wikipedia. https://commons.wikimedia.org/w/index.php?curid=20516824.

(2015). *Autodromo Hermanos Rodriguez 2015*. Mexico City. [Own work]. In Wikipedia. https://commons.wikimedia.org/w/index.php?curid=38939156.

Pittenger, W. (2008). *Formula1 Circuit Catalunya*. Spain. [Own work]. In Wikipedia. Retrieved from https://commons.wikimedia.org/w/index.php?curid=4505005.

(2008). *Hungaroring*. Hungary. [Own work]. In Wikipedia. Retrieved from https://commons.wikimedia.org/w/index.php?curid=4473986.

(2008). *Monza track map Formula1.com map*. Italy. [Own work]. In Wikipedia. https://commons.wikimedia.org/w/index.php?curid=4788200.

(2008). *Losail International Circuit in Qatar*. [Own work]. In Wikipedia. Retrieved from https://commons.wikimedia.org/wiki/File:Losail.svg.

(2009). *Monte Carlo Formula1 track map*. Monaco. [Own work]. In Wikipedia. https://commons.wikimedia.org/w/index.php?curid=7889892.

(2009*). Spa-Francorchamps of Belgium*. [Own work].In Wikipedia. https://commons.wikimedia.org/w/index.php?curid=7699160.

(2009*). Suzuka Circuit Map – 2005*. Japan. [Own work]. In Wikipedia. Retrieved from https://commons.wikimedia.org/w/index.php?curid=8986552.

(2010). *Albert Lake Park Street Circuit in Melbourne, Australia.* [Own work]. In Wikipedia.
https://commons.wikimedia.org/w/index.php?curid=10595994.

(2010). *Bahrain International Circuit—Grand Prix Layout.* Bahrain. [Own work]. In Wikipedia.
https://commons.wikimedia.org/wiki/File:Bahrain_International_Circuit--Grand_Prix_Layout.svg.

Pucking. (2021). *Racing Icon Set in Thin Line Style.* [Vector Image]. Shutterstock. Retrieved from https://www.shutterstock.com/image-vector/racing-icon-set-thin-line-style-593297576.

Scarborough, C. and Windsor Clarke, P. (2022). *F1 Floor Dramas: Scarb's Analysis with Peter Windsor on Twitch/TV.* [Video Stream]. YouTube. Retrieved 02/14/23 from https://www.youtube.com/watch?v=R__GCcSmzuM.

Sentoan. (2011*). Imola 2009.* Emilia Romagna. [Own work]. (2011, In Wikipedia. https://commons.wikimedia.org/w/index.php?curid=14323726.

(2016). *Autodromo de Algarve.* Portugal. [Derivative work]. In Wikipedia. https://commons.wikimedia.org/w/index.php?curid=54225186.

Stefanphotozemun. (2022). *Sport Race Car Blueprint – 3D Perspective Formula One.* [Vector Image]. Shutterstock. Retrieved from https://www.shutterstock.com/image-illustration/sport-race-car-blueprint-3d-perspective-595622498.

The Athletic Staff. (2022). *Formula 1 Viewership: 2022 Season Sets U.S. Record, viewership Up 34% Among Women.* [Article]. The Athletic.com. Retrieved 03/12/2023 from https://theathletic.com/3924843/2022/11/23/formula-1-viewership-2022/.

We hope that you are happy with your purchase of

FORMULA 1 HANDBOOK 2023

Grand Prix Guide for F1 Fans

and that it has revvvvved up your experience of this year's racing.

If by any chance the book you have received is damaged or defective,

you may return it to Amazon within 30 days of purchase

for a replacement or refund.

We would really appreciate it if you left an honest review

on Amazon at your earliest convenience using your country's link at:

http://www.amazon.com/review/create-review?&asin= 0645666718

http://www.amazon.co.uk/review/create-review?&asin= 0645666718

http://www.amazon.com.au/review/create-review?&asin= 0645666718

http://www.amazon.ca/review/create-review?&asin= 0645666718

or by scanning one of these QR codes:

US	UK	AUS	CAN

You can also check out our other books at:

amazon.com/author/epic-wordsmiths_4_an_epic-life

Made in the USA
Las Vegas, NV
26 September 2023

78180001R00079